100

GREAT QUESTIONS

FOR DEEP CONVERSATIONS

DAVID PARIS

ILLUSTRATED BY JOSEPH SHEPHERD

ACKNOWLEDGEMENTS

I am immensely grateful to my brother, Ben Paris, who brought his training in critical thinking and instructional design to the book from beginning to end (find him at BenParisTestPrep.com). He is brilliant and I am lucky to have him as my brother.

Thank you Joseph Shepherd for bringing visual life to these questions. Your artistry is inspiring.

Thank you Oksana Kosovan for your beautiful formatting.

Thank you to all of the teenagers from around the world who answered the questions and were willing to share their responses in this book.

And thank you Gaston Braun, for funding this project. You set the example for curiosity and inquisitiveness for all of us. You are profoundly missed.

INTRODUCTION

100 Great Questions for Deep Conversations is a collection of the most popular questions from 1000 Social Emotional Questions. The book is an adventure for the mind and a catalyst for dialogue. Each question will inspire reflection and discussion. You will get to compare your answers with responses with your friends and family, as well as with teenagers from all over the world. Enjoy the journey. A deep, engaging conversation awaits.

'IF YOU MADE UP YOUR OWN NATIONAL HOLIDAY,
WHAT WOULD IT BE AND HOW WOULD WE CELEBRATE?'

1 IF YOU MADE UP YOUR OWN NATIONAL HOLIDAY, WHAT WOULD IT BE AND HOW WOULD WE CELEBRATE?

A. Yes Day. Adults have to say yes to everything. (Demetri, Ukraine)

B. National Relax Day. No one would do anything. Everyone would wear pajamas all day long. (Lisa, U.S.A)

C. Be Nice Day. Everyone would have to go out of their way to be kind to each other. (Nzemeke, Nigeria)

Your Answer

Friend or Family Answer

2 WHAT IS YOUR FAVORITE HOLIDAY AND WHY?

A. Halloween. We get to wear costumes and eat lots of candy. (Kiera, U.S.A)

B. Eid is my favorite holiday because we wear traditional clothes and eat amazing food. (Betu, Turkey)

C. New Year's Day. I love yelling, "Happy New Year" and I don't get in trouble for yelling. (Brandon, U.S.A)

Your Answer

Friend or Family Answer

'IF YOU COULD HAVE ANY VIEW FROM YOUR BEDROOM
WINDOW, WHAT WOULD IT BE?'

8

3 IF YOU COULD HAVE ANY VIEW FROM YOUR BEDROOM WINDOW, WHAT WOULD IT BE?

A. I would like to have a view on a big mountain with snowy peaks. (George, U.S.A)

B. An apple orchard. (Sophie, France)

C. A view of the entire city from the 99th floor. (Betu, Turkey)

Your Answer

Friend or Family Answer

4 IF YOU COULD PAINT A MURAL ON YOUR BED-ROOM CEILING, WHAT WOULD YOU PUT ON IT?

A. I would include the moon, the sea, and a lot of flowers. (Niyoosha, Pakistan)

B. The world map or maybe the solar system. (Zaidh, Kenya)

C. A soccer field. (August, U.S.A)

Your Answer

Friend or Family Answer

'IF YOU COULD CREATE A MOVIE,
WHAT GENRE WOULD IT BE?'

5 IF YOU COULD CREATE A MOVIE, WHAT GENRE WOULD IT BE?

A. Comedy. (Lilliana, U.S.A.)

B. Action. (Javier, Mexico)

C. Fantasy. (Yennifer, Dominican Republic)

Your Answer

Friend or Family Answer

6 WHAT ACTOR WOULD STAR IN THE FILM AND WHAT WOULD IT BE ABOUT?

A. Kevin Hart. Someone who loses their memory and says what they really think. (Etienne, France)

B. Dwayne Johnson. The film would be a modern adaptation of Othello turned into a mafia story. (Niyoosha, Pakistan)

C. Jennifer Lawrence. The main character is a time traveler who uses her power selfishly. (Yennifer, Dominican Republic)

Your Answer

Friend or Family Answer

'IF YOU COULD HAVE FOUR DINNER GUESTS, LIVING OR DEAD, REAL OR FICTIONAL, WHO WOULD THEY BE?'

7 IF YOU COULD HAVE FOUR DINNER GUESTS, LIVING OR DEAD, REAL OR FICTIONAL, WHO WOULD THEY BE?

A. Snoop Dogg, Kevin Hart, my geography teacher, and my best friend Sonia. (Milka, Montenegro)

B. Steve Harvey, my grandma, Michael Jackson, Barack Obama. (Evan, U.S.A)

C. Harry Styles, Doja Cat, Spiderman, and Harry Potter. (Javier, Mexico.)

Your Answer

Friend or Family Answer

8 WHAT FOOD WOULD YOU SERVE?

A. Pizza, brownies, and sliders. (Lisa, U.S.A)

B. Homemade ugalis, kale and beef. (Mywangi, Kenya)

C. Only desserts. (Etienne, France)

Your Answer

Friend or Family Answer

'IF YOU COULD DESIGN A FLOAT FOR A PARADE, WHAT
WOULD YOU MAKE AND WHO WOULD BE ON THE FLOAT?'

9

IF YOU COULD DESIGN A FLOAT FOR A PARADE, WHAT WOULD YOU MAKE AND WHO WOULD BE ON THE FLOAT?

A. A collage of novels. (Ushim, South Africa)

B. A fairy enchanted forest float. (Sophie, France)

C. A sailboat with my friend on it. (Evan, U.S.A)

Your Answer

Friend or Family Answer

10

WHICH PARADES WOULD YOU ATTEND?

A. Mermaid parade (Violet, U.S.A.)

B. Halloween Parade (Liz, U.S.A)

C. Carnival in Rio de Janeiro (Heitor, Brazil)

Your Answer

Friend or Family Answer

'IN WHAT WAYS DO PEOPLE MISJUDGE YOU?'

11 IN WHAT WAYS DO PEOPLE MISJUDGE YOU?

A. Whenever I am quiet, people always assume I am bored with their conversations. (Nusrat, Bangladesh)

B. I seem to be rude and a mean girl, but I think that's just how I look. (Anastasia, U.S.A)

C. When I'm making other people smile, but actually I am not happy inside. (Miu, Japan)

Your Answer

Friend or Family Answer

12 WHEN DO YOU FEEL UNDERSTOOD?

A. I recently shared with my sister that my math teacher picks on me. My sister opened up and said that she also had the same experience. (Milka, Montenegro.)

B. When someone listens to music with me and we both get the vibe. (Niko, Netherlands)

C. When I talk to my dad. (Evan, U.S.A.)

Your Answer

Friend or Family Answer

'ARE YOU AN OPTIMIST, PESSIMIST, OR REALIST?'

13 ARE YOU AN OPTIMIST, PESSIMIST, OR REALIST?

A. Realist. (Milka, Montenegro)

B. Optimist. (Ushim, South Africa)

C. Pessimist and realist. (Rocky, U.S.A)

Your Answer

Friend or Family Answer

14 WHAT ARE YOU OPTIMISTIC, PESSIMISTIC OR REALISTIC ABOUT?

A. I am optimistic that if I get good grades, I will get into a great college. (Kyra, U.S.A.)

B. I am pessimistic about climate change. (Etienne, France)

C. I am realistic about finances. (Xiomarys, Puerto Rico)

Your Answer

Friend or Family Answer

'IF YOU COULD GO BACK IN TIME AND GIVE YOUR YOUNGER SELF ADVICE, WHAT WOULD YOU TELL YOURSELF?'

15 IF YOU COULD GO BACK IN TIME AND GIVE YOUR YOUNGER SELF ADVICE, WHAT WOULD YOU TELL YOURSELF?

A. Start saving money for a phone. (Rocky, U.S.A.)

B. I'd tell my younger self to not worry too much about being liked. (Mywangi, Kenya)

C. Appreciate and love herself more. (Sophie, France)

Your Answer

Friend or Family Answer

16 IF YOU COULD GO FORWARD IN TIME AND GIVE YOUR OLDER SELF ADVICE, WHAT WOULD YOU TELL YOURSELF?

A. Don't do anything stupid. (Niko, Netherlands)

B. Work hard and make money. (George, U.S.A)

C. I would tell myself to not forget what my younger self had wanted. (Ushim, South Africa)

Your Answer

Friend or Family Answer

'WHAT'S THE BEST AND HARDEST PART
ABOUT BEING YOUR AGE?'

17 WHAT'S THE BEST AND HARDEST PART ABOUT BEING YOUR AGE?

A. I have more freedom now, but I also have more responsibility. (Kyra, U.S.A.)

B. The best part is not having to pay your own bills. The worst part is not having your own money and having to ask for things that you want. (Kim, South Korea)

C. The best part about being my age is the new intensity of emotions I feel. This is also the hardest part. (Ushim, South Africa)

Your Answer

Friend or Family Answer

18 WHAT ADVICE WOULD YOU GIVE SOMEONE RAISING SOMEONE YOUR AGE?

A. Allow us to make mistakes because through mistakes, we learn. (Pavan, India.)

B. Let us participate in decision-making. (Milka, Montenegro)

C. We may frustrate you so much, but we appreciate you more than you know. (Lisa, U.S.A.)

Your Answer

Friend or Family Answer

'WHAT DOES EVERYONE HAVE TO LEARN THAT YOU FEEL IS USELESS?'

19 WHAT DOES EVERYONE HAVE TO LEARN THAT YOU FEEL IS USELESS?

A. Geometry. (Liliana, U.S.A)

B. Ancient civilizations. (Heitor, Brazil)

C. Insect biology. (Mywangi, Kenya)

Your Answer

Friend or Family Answer

20 WHAT IS CRUCIAL TO LEARN?

A. How to make money. (Rocky, U.S.A)

B. I think everyone should learn communication skills. (Angel, U.S.A.)

C. Planets and galaxies. (Betul, Turkey)

Your Answer

Friend or Family Answer

'IF YOUR LIFE WERE A MOVIE AND YOU WERE IN CHARGE
OF THE SOUNDTRACK, WHAT MUSIC WOULD YOU USE?'

21 IF YOUR LIFE WERE A MOVIE AND YOU WERE IN CHARGE OF THE SOUNDTRACK, WHAT MUSIC WOULD YOU USE?

A. When I am happy: Sweet Child of Mine by Guns and Roses. (George, U.S.A.)

B. When I fail at something: Begin Again by Zayn. (Sophie, France)

C. In a tense situation: the Game of Thrones soundtrack. (Milka, Montenegro)

Your Answer

Friend or Family Answer

22 WHAT IS ONE SONG YOU NEVER GET TIRED OF?

A. Can't Stop the Feeling by Justin Timberlake. (Lilliana, U.S.A)

B. El Cantante (Xiomarys, Puerto Rico)

C. Baby Shark (Evan, U.S.A.)

Your Answer

Friend or Family Answer

'HOW WOULD LIFE BE DIFFERENT IF WE KNEW EACH
OTHER'S THOUGHTS?'

23 HOW WOULD LIFE BE DIFFERENT IF WE KNEW EACH OTHER'S THOUGHTS?

A. We'd be able to predict each other's actions. (Nusrat, Bangladesh)

B. Nobody would have to pretend anymore. (Javier, Mexico)

C. No more dishonesty. (George, U.S.A.)

Your Answer

Friend or Family Answer

24 YOU HAVE TELEPATHY FOR 24 HOURS, HOW DO YOU USE IT?

A. I'd go visit all the presidents in the world. (Sophie, France)

B. I would try to find out who are really my best friends and spend some time with them. (Lilliana, U.S.A)

C. Poker. (Evan, U.S.A)

Your Answer

Friend or Family Answer

'IF YOU COULD CREATE A PORTAL BETWEEN ANY TWO PLACES ON EARTH, WHICH PLACES WOULD YOU CHOOSE?'

25 IF YOU COULD CREATE A PORTAL BETWEEN ANY TWO PLACES ON EARTH, WHICH PLACES WOULD YOU CHOOSE?

A. I would make a portal between Disney World and Universal. (George, U.S.A.)

B. I would choose to have a portal between my room and a place where my father lives and works. That way we could see each other faster. (Betul, Turkey)

C. I would choose a portal between my kitchen and my favorite vegan restaurant. (Violet, U.S.A)

Your Answer

Friend or Family Answer

26 WHAT IF THE PORTAL WAS ONE-WAY?

A. Just between my house and school, so that I could sleep longer in the morning. (Kiera, U.S.A)

B. I would choose a portal between the bottom and top of a mountain, so I could always go downhill. (Brandon, U.S.A.)

C. A one-way portal to the South Pole. That way I could get rid of all my enemies. (Ettiene, France)

Your Answer

Friend or Family Answer

'WHAT NEW TECHNOLOGY DO YOU WANT INVENTED?'

27 WHAT NEW TECHNOLOGY DO YOU WANT INVENTED?

A. Transportation without pollution. (Javier, Mexico)

B. A machine that helps you with your house chores. (Zaidh, Nigeria)

C. A google brain chip. (Milka, Montenegro)

Your Answer

Friend or Family Answer

28 IS TECHNOLOGICAL PROGRESS ALWAYS GOOD? WHY OR WHY NOT?

A. Technological progress isn't always good. The more we progress, the lazier and more reliant we become. (Ushim, South Africa)

B. Through technology, scientists could share knowledge and discoveries that would help curb the spread of disease. (Nyawira, Kenya)

C. Technology can be good when it helps with major human problems, but it can also harm the environment. (Niyoosha, Pakistan)

Your Answer

Friend or Family Answer

'IMAGINE YOU CAN CREATE ANY ONE LAW,
WHAT LAW WOULD YOU CREATE?'

29 IMAGINE YOU CAN CREATE ANY ONE LAW, WHAT LAW WOULD YOU CREATE?

A. No school after noon time. (Rocky, U.S.A.)

B. No one could be mean to animals. (Kiera, U.S.A.)

C. To ask as many questions as I want without being told to be quiet. (Heitor, Brazil)

Your Answer

Friend or Family Answer

30 WHAT LAW WOULD YOU CHANGE?

A. People can move freely to whichever part of the world they want. (Alicia, South Africa)

B. Kids can vote. (Lilliana, U.S.A)

C. Gun laws. (George, U.S.A.)

Your Answer

Friend or Family Answer

'IF YOU COULD RID THE WORLD OF ONE EMOTION,
WHAT EMOTION WOULD YOU GET RID OF AND WHY?'

31 IF YOU COULD RID THE WORLD OF ONE EMOTION, WHAT EMOTION WOULD YOU GET RID OF AND WHY?

A. Greed. (Sophie, France)

B. Hate. That's why people do bad things. (Zaidh, Nigeria)

C. Anger, it makes you do impulsive stuff. (Kim, South Korea)

Your Answer

Friend or Family Answer

32 IF YOU COULD HAVE PEOPLE CONNECT TO ONE EMOTION MORE, WHICH WOULD YOU CHOOSE? WHY?

A. Appreciation. (Lisa, U.S.A.)

B. Happiness. (Hector, Brazil)

C. Love. That's why people do good things. (Zaidh, Nigeria)

Your Answer

Friend or Family Answer

'WHO HAS SHAPED THE WAY YOU SEE THE WORLD?
HOW HAVE THEY INFLUENCED YOU?'

33

WHO HAS SHAPED THE WAY YOU SEE THE WORLD? HOW HAVE THEY INFLUENCED YOU?

A. Messi. He taught me to never give up, no matter what your circumstances. (Kyla, U.S.A.)

B. My mom. She is kind and generous. I have learned how to be loving. (Zaidh, Nigeria)

C. My friends. They make sure I don't get a big head. (Angel, U.S.A.)

Your Answer

Friend or Family Answer

34

WHO HAVE YOU INFLUENCED? IN WHAT WAYS HAVE YOU INFLUENCED THEM?

A. My younger sister. I showed her how to be kind and open-minded. (Niyoosha, Pakistan)

B. My dog. He learned how to sit, but he still licks me too much. (George, U.S.A)

C. My friend Yasmine. She was really down on herself, but I always told her she's special. (Lisa, U.S.A)

Your Answer

Friend or Family Answer

'ON A SCALE OF 1-10,
HOW MUCH OF A PERFECTIONIST ARE YOU?'

35 ON A SCALE OF 1-10, HOW MUCH OF A PERFECTIONIST ARE YOU?

A. I am a 5. Sometimes I work at things until they're perfect, sometimes I just want to move on to something else. (Javier, Mexico)

B. I am a 10 because I won't stop until everything is perfect. (Kiera, U.S.A.)

C. It depends on my mood and how invested I am in what I am doing. (Sophie, France)

Your Answer

Friend or Family Answer

36 HOW DO YOU KNOW WHETHER A TASK IS DONE OR NEEDS MORE ATTENTION?

A. My mom tells me. (Gus, U.S.A.)

B. I listen to my intuition. (Pavan, India)

C. I evaluate what I did and what was expected of me. (Nzemeke, Nigeria)

Your Answer

Friend or Family Answer

'WHAT DO YOU FIND RUDE?'

37 WHAT DO YOU FIND RUDE?

A. People who cut in line. (Betul, Turkey)

B. I find it rude when people make you feel left out or ignored. (Anastasia, U.S.A.)

C. When people interrupt me. (Niko, Netherlands)

Your Answer

Friend or Family Answer

38 WHAT DO YOU DO THAT OTHERS FIND RUDE?

A. My friend at school says that I chew my food loudly. (George, U.S.A.)

B. I don't know when to keep quiet. (Mywangi, Kenya)

C. Sometimes, my sarcasm and humor comes across as rude. (Heitor, Brazil)

Your Answer

Friend or Family Answer

'WHEN HAVE YOU MADE A JUDGMENT ABOUT SOMEONE
THAT WAS TOTALLY WRONG?'

39 WHEN HAVE YOU MADE A JUDGMENT ABOUT SOMEONE THAT WAS TOTALLY WRONG?

A. I saw this girl with dyed hair and I thought she was crazy. But she was actually just like me when I got to know her. (Kyla, U.S.A.)

B. A new kid came into the class and there was mean gossip about him. Turns out none of it was true. (Jaime, Australia)

C. My sister didn't tell me about a party and I was mad. However, it turns out she did try to tell me and then I felt bad. (Sophie, France)

Your Answer

Friend or Family Answer

40 WHEN ARE JUDGMENTS USEFUL AND WHEN ARE THEY NOT?

A. Judgements are useful when we are trying to figure out what is better for ourselves, but they are not useful when we are judging someone based on the way they look. (Niyoosha, Pakistan)

B. Judgments are okay if you are not fixed on your thinking. (Nzemeke, Kenya)

C. Judgments are useful when you have detailed and accurate facts. (Eduardo, Peru)

Your Answer

Friend or Family Answer

'WHEN ARE YOU THE HAPPIEST?'

41 WHEN ARE YOU THE HAPPIEST?

A. Playing soccer. (Kyra, U.S.A.)

B. When my parents are proud of me. (Zaidh, Nigeria)

C. When I am eating. (Niko, Netherlands)

Your Answer

Friend or Family Answer

42 WHAT CAN YOU DO TO BRING MORE HAPPINESS INTO YOUR LIFE?

A. Avoid stress. (Javier, Mexico)

B. Enjoy the small things in life. (Niyoosha, Pakistan)

C. Join a dance crew. (Kiera, U.S.A.)

Your Answer

Friend or Family Answer

'WHAT HABIT WOULD YOU LIKE TO MAKE?'

43 WHAT HABIT WOULD YOU LIKE TO MAKE?

A. Waking up on time. (Nusrat, Bangladesh)

B. Reading 30 minutes a day. (Nzemeke, Nigeria)

C. To do a flip on the trampoline every day. (George, U.S.A.)

Your Answer

Friend or Family Answer

44 WHAT IS A HABIT YOU WANT TO BREAK?

A. Overthinking. (Eduardo, Peru)

B. Procrastination. (Xiomarys, Puerto Rico)

C. Thinking I am not good enough to do something. (Anastasia, U.S.A.)

Your Answer

Friend or Family Answer

'WHAT CAN WE LEARN FROM OLDER GENERATIONS?'

45 WHAT CAN WE LEARN FROM OLDER GENERATIONS?

A. Stories from history. (Niko, Netherlands)

B. How things were harder in the past. (Miu, Japan)

C. How to survive. (George, U.S.A.)

Your Answer

Friend or Family Answer

46 WHAT DO YOU WANT TO TEACH TO FUTURE GENERATIONS?

A. How to love others unconditionally. (Sophie, France)

B. When things stop working out, ask for help. (Xiomarys, Puerto Rico)

C. To unlearn the cycles of abuse and misogyny that have been internalized over the past generations. (Alicia, South Africa)

Your Answer

Friend or Family Answer

'HOW HAVE YOU OVERCOME A MISTAKE?'

47 HOW HAVE YOU OVERCOME A MISTAKE?

A. I ate all of my friend's chips, so I bought him a new bag the next day. (George, U.S.A.)

B. I said something mean to my mom. I realized I was wrong later and I apologized. (Sophie, France)

C. I once lost my cell phone. Now I am more careful. (Kim, South Korea)

Your Answer

Friend or Family Answer

48 WHAT'S THE WORST MISTAKE YOU'VE EVER MADE?

A. I once left my sister's birthday cake alone in the kitchen with my dog and he ate it. (Nzemeke, Nigeria)

B. I broke my mother's vase. I tried to put it back together, but she noticed the cracks. (Javier, Mexico)

C. I got back together with my boyfriend after he dumped me. And then he dumped me again. (Lilliana, U.S.A.)

Your Answer

Friend or Family Answer

'WHEN HAVE YOU CHANGED SOMEONE'S MIND AND HOW DID YOU DO IT?'

49 WHEN HAVE YOU CHANGED SOMEONE'S MIND AND HOW DID YOU DO IT?

A. I have changed my sister's mind for a vacation by listing pros and cons. (Ushim, South Africa)

B. When I wanted special lights for my room and my parents said no, I begged. (Lisa, U.S.A.)

C. I changed someone's mind when my friend wasn't going to watch a show, but I made them watch the first episode with me. Then they got hooked. (Niko, Netherlands)

Your Answer

Friend or Family Answer

50 WHEN HAS SOMEONE CHANGED YOUR MIND AND HOW DID THEY DO IT?

A. When I was going to straighten my hair, my friend said my natural curls look good. So I kept it curly. (Vicky, U.S.A)

B. I didn't like Nirvana, but my dad told me a little about them, which built my curiosity. (Alicia, South Africa)

C. I didn't want to go camping, but my mom asked me to just try it. I did it for one night and I actually enjoyed it. (Ettienne, France)

Your Answer

Friend or Family Answer

'IF YOU COULD HAVE A PORTABLE CAR HORN TO WARN
PEOPLE, WHAT WOULD YOU USE IT FOR?'

51

IF YOU COULD HAVE A PORTABLE CAR HORN TO WARN PEOPLE, WHAT WOULD YOU USE IT FOR?

A. I'd use it to make room for older people to pass on the sidewalk. (Zaidh, Nigeria)

B. I'd use the portable car horn to warn people when I'm angry so they'll know to avoid me. (Jaime, Australia)

C. I'd use it to wake me up in the morning. (Kiera and Kyla, U..S.A.)

Your Answer

Friend or Family Answer

52

IF YOU COULD HAVE A SPEAKER BLAST A MESSAGE REPEATEDLY THROUGHOUT THE DAY, WHAT WOULD IT SAY?

A. You look beautiful today. (Niyoosha, Pakistan)

B. Nothing is impossible. (Niko, Netherlands)

C. Back away. (Brandon, U.S.A.)

Your Answer

Friend or Family Answer

'WHAT MAKES A GOOD FRIEND?'

53 WHAT MAKES A GOOD FRIEND?

A. A friend who is always there for you, respects your opinions, but also lets you know when you're wrong. (Pavan, India)

B. A good friend is willing to listen to your stupid jokes and laugh about them. They love you for who you are. (Xiomarys, Puerto Rico)

C. Loyalty. (George, U.S.A.)

Your Answer

Friend or Family Answer

54 HOW ARE YOU A "GOOD FRIEND?"

A. I am kind to my friends and make them laugh. (Javier, Mexico)

B. I try to be there for people when they need me and don't hold grudges. (Ettienne, France)

C. I am easy to talk to and I speak the truth. (Anastasia, U.S.A.)

Your Answer

Friend or Family Answer

'WHAT GETS ON YOUR NERVES?'

55   WHAT GETS ON YOUR NERVES?

A. When somebody has a hard time seeing things from my perspective, I feel frustrated, (Betu, Turkey)

B. It gets on my nerves when people probe me about something I don't want to talk about. (Niyoosha, Pakistan)

C. False accusations and lies get on my nerves. (Lisa, U.S.A.)

Your Answer

Friend or Family Answer

56   HOW DO YOU CALM YOUR NERVES?

A. Deep breaths. (Eduardo, Peru)

B. Hugging my dog. (Kierra, U.S.A)

C. I just let it all out. (Sophie, France)

Your Answer

Friend or Family Answer

'WHEN LIFE GAVE YOU LEMONS, WHEN DID YOU MAKE LEMONADE?'

57   WHEN LIFE GAVE YOU LEMONS, WHEN DID YOU MAKE LEMONADE?

A. I had hoped to represent my school in a major competition, but I was not chosen. I helped my friend who was selected and he won. I was proud. (Milka, Montenegro)

B. When I got involved in a car accident. I was home a lot. I learned how to study independently. (Etienne, France)

C. When my XBOX burned, I learned to play games on the mobile phone. Now I can play video games anywhere. (Ushim, South Africa)

Your Answer

Friend or Family Answer

58   WHEN HAVE YOU ACHIEVED SOMETHING THAT SEEMED IMPOSSIBLE?

A. Sometimes, video games seem impossible to finish, but there is always a way. (Niko, Netherlands)

B. I learned how to play guitar. It took a year! (Javier, Mexico)

C. I made it to my school's dance team even though I had never taken a dance class before. (Xlomarys, Puerto Rico)

Your Answer

Friend or Family Answer

'DOES IT MATTER IF SOMEONE DOES SOMETHING
WRONG IF NO ONE EVER KNOWS ABOUT IT?'

59 DOES IT MATTER IF SOMEONE DOES SOMETHING WRONG IF NO ONE EVER KNOWS ABOUT IT?

A. Yes, people should have integrity. (Nzemeke, Nigeria)

B. If no one ever knows, then is it really wrong? (Ushim, South Africa)

C. If someone is hurt, then it matters. (Miu, Japan)

Your Answer

Friend or Family Answer

60 HOW DO YOU RESOLVE DISAGREEMENTS ABOUT MORALITY?

A. I try to understand another person's perspective and I hope that they then try to understand my perspective. (Pavan, India)

B. I try to prove them wrong about what is right. (Eduardo, Peru)

C. I pray for them. (Yennifer, Dominican Republic)

Your Answer

Friend or Family Answer

'IF YOU HAD A REMOTE THAT CONTROLLED THE WORLD, HOW WOULD YOU USE IT?'

61 IF YOU HAD A REMOTE THAT CONTROLLED THE WORLD, HOW WOULD YOU USE IT?

A. I would mute people. (George, U.S.A.)

B. I would change the channel when I was bored. (Niko, Netherlands)

C. I'd use the remote control to prevent people from starting wars. (Ushim, South Africa)

Your Answer

Friend or Family Answer

62 IF YOU HAD ONLY ONE BUTTON, WHICH WOULD YOU CHOOSE AND WHAT WOULD YOU DO WITH IT?

A. I'd pause the bad people. (Zaidh, Nigeria)

B. To fast forward and see how the world looks in 100 years. (Etienne, France)

C. I'd press power off and see what happens. (Brandon, U.S.A.)

Your Answer

Friend or Family Answer

'IF YOU HAD TO REPEAT A DAY AGAIN AND AGAIN,
WHAT DAY WOULD YOU REPEAT?'

63 IF YOU HAD TO REPEAT A DAY AGAIN AND AGAIN, WHAT DAY WOULD YOU REPEAT?

A. My 13th birthday. It was so much fun. (Nusrat, Bangladesh)

B. The day I won an award for best student at my school. (Zaidh, Nigeria)

C. Any Saturday. It's the best day of the week, (Niko, Netherlands)

Your Answer

Friend or Family Answer

64 WHAT YEAR WOULD YOU WANT TO REPEAT?

A. I would repeat last year because I sat next to my best friend in school. (Kyla, U.S.A)

B. Last year because I vacationed in Cairo. (Betu, Turkey)

C. The year I was born. (Nzemeke, Kenya)

Your Answer

Friend or Family Answer

'IF YOU COULD CHOOSE ONE SUPERPOWER,
WHAT WOULD YOU CHOOSE?'

65 IF YOU COULD CHOOSE ONE SUPERPOWER, WHAT WOULD YOU CHOOSE?

A. Shapeshifting. (Brandon, U.S.A.)

B. Speaking to the dead. (Miu, Japan)

C. To heal people through touch. (Nusrat, Bangladesh)

Your Answer

Friend or Family Answer

66 WHAT SUPERPOWER WOULD YOU CHOOSE IF YOU WERE TRYING TO MAKE THE WORLD BETTER IN SOME WAY?

A. Mind control, so I could change the thoughts of people who do negative things. (Dana, Canada)

B. Teleport people who are in danger. (Javier, Mexico)

C. The power of super-recycling. (Violet, U.S.A.)

Your Answer

Friend or Family Answer

'WHO SUPPORTS YOU IN YOUR LIFE AND HOW?'

67 WHO SUPPORTS YOU IN YOUR LIFE AND HOW?

A. My friends and family. They help me solve my problems and cheer me up when I am sad. (Angel, U.S.A.)

B. My sisters help me make decisions and believe in me. (Niyoosha, Pakistan)

C. My teachers are always there to help when I am confused. (Dana, Canada)

Your Answer

Friend or Family Answer

68 WHAT SUPPORT WOULD YOU LIKE THAT YOU ARE NOT GETTING NOW?

A. I would like to have more emotional support. (Lilliana, U.S.A)

B. I'd like to take classes so I can be a web developer. (Eduardo, Peru)

C. I need help motivating myself. Sometimes I don't feel like doing anything. (Etienne, France)

Your Answer

Friend or Family Answer

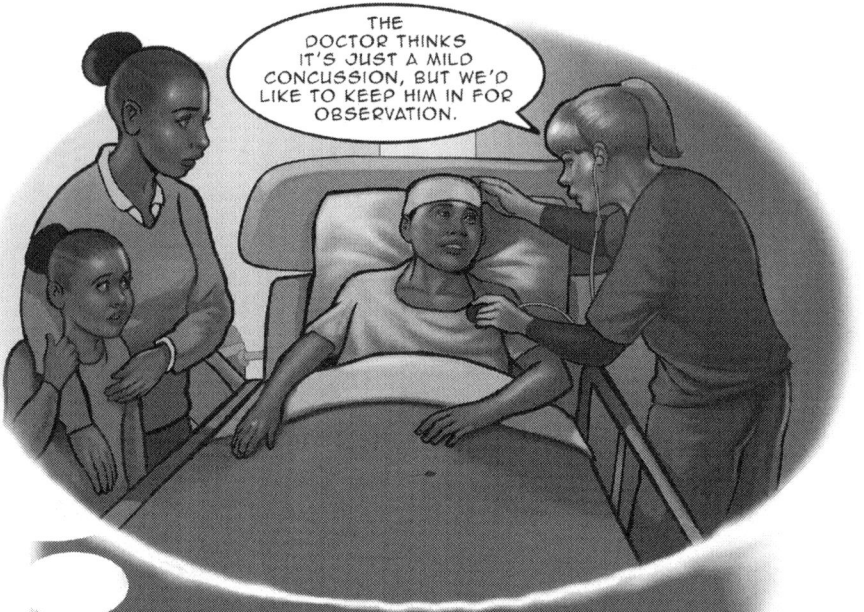

'WHAT WAS THE LONGEST DAY OF YOUR LIFE, AND WHY?'

69 WHAT WAS THE LONGEST DAY OF YOUR LIFE, AND WHY?

A. I had to take a five-hour test for high school. (Nzemeke, Kenya)

B. I was hospitalized because my appendix burst. It was really scary. (Zaidh, Nigeria)

C. There was a storm and I was stuck by myself at home. (Lisa, U.S.A.)

Your Answer

Friend or Family Answer

70 WHAT IS THE BEST WAY TO GET THROUGH HARD TIMES?

A. Talking to your friends. (Niko, Netherlands)

B. Have faith and believe that tough times don't last. (Javier, Mexico)

C. Take one step at a time. (Betu, Turkey)

Your Answer

Friend or Family Answer

'DO YOU OFTEN COMPARE YOURSELF TO OTHERS?'

71 DO YOU OFTEN COMPARE YOURSELF TO OTHERS?

A. Sometimes. (Dana, Canada)

B. All the time. (Xiomarys, Puerto Rico)

C. Yes, but I try not to. (Sophie, France)

Your Answer

Friend or Family Answer

72 IS IT HELPFUL OR HARMFUL?

A. Comparing myself to others is helpful because it makes me push myself to be the best I can be. (Alicia, South Africa)

B. It is harmful because it makes you second guess yourself. (Lilliana, U.S.A.)

C. Sometimes it's motivating, something it's deflating. (Eduardo, Peru)

Your Answer

Friend or Family Answer

'WHO WAS YOUR FAVORITE TEACHER AND WHY?'

73 WHO WAS YOUR FAVORITE TEACHER AND WHY?

A. My literature teacher was my favorite teacher because she was funny and told great stories. (George, U.S.A.)

B. Mr. Wankiku taught me very difficult math. (Nzemeke, Kenya)

C. My kindergarten teacher was my favorite because I got a hug every day. (Xiomarys, Puerto Rico)

Your Answer

Friend or Family Answer

74 WHAT MAKES A GREAT TEACHER?

A. A teacher who understands and supports you. (Angel, U.S.A.)

B. Someone who listens, adapts, sets an example, and knows what they are teaching. (Zaidh, Nigeria)

C. A great teacher is someone who is accessible, makes their students feel comfortable, gives all of their students equal attention, and can communicate. (Niyoosha, Pakistan)

Your Answer

Friend or Family Answer

'IF YOU COULD BE ANY ANIMAL,
WHAT WOULD YOU BE AND WHY?'

75 IF YOU COULD BE ANY ANIMAL, WHAT WOULD YOU BE AND WHY?

A. I would like to be a bird because they fly freely in the sky. (Kim, South Korea)

B. I'd be a dolphin. They are beautiful, kind, and intelligent. (Yennifer, Dominican Republic)

C. I'd be a panda because they are rare and herbivores. (Violet, U.S.A.)

Your Answer

Friend or Family Answer

76 IF YOU HAD TO SPEND A WEEK AS ONE TYPE OF PLANT, WHAT PLANT WOULD YOU BE?

A. A Venus flytrap. (Brandon, U.S.A.)

B. A stink plant so no one would eat me. (Niko, Netherlands)

C. I would be a rose. A red rose. It is my mother's favorite color and flower. (Nzemeke, Kenya)

Your Answer

Friend or Family Answer

'WHAT DO YOU NEED MORE OF RIGHT NOW?'

77 WHAT DO YOU NEED MORE OF RIGHT NOW?

A. I need more sleep. (Angel, U.S.A.)

B. I need more friends as I recently moved and I don't know a lot of people out here. (Niyoosha, Pakistan)

C. I need more self-esteem, (Zaidh, Nigeria)

Your Answer

Friend or Family Answer

78 WHAT DO YOU NEED LESS OF?

A. Stress, I want to reduce my stress level. (Lisa, U.S.A.)

B. Guilt. (Noah, U.S.A.)

C. Distractions. Less social media as it wastes a lot of my time. (Javier, Mexico)

Your Answer

Friend or Family Answer

'WHAT NEW PUNCTUATION WOULD YOU CREATE IF
EVERYONE HAD TO LEARN IT?'

79 WHAT NEW PUNCTUATION WOULD YOU CREATE IF EVERYONE HAD TO LEARN IT?

A. I would create a heart (<3). (Lisa, U.S.A.)

B. I would create two ellipses to indicate a long wait.
   (Etienne, France)

C. I would use the number 2 to tell people to read the sentence again.
   (Pavan, India)

Your Answer

Friend or Family Answer

80 WHAT WORD SHOULD ALWAYS BE CAPITALIZED?

A. Cupcakes. (Brandon, U.S.A)

B. Love. (Javier, Mexico)

C. GOAL!. (Etienne, France)

Your Answer

Friend or Family Answer

'WHAT MOTIVATES YOU?'

81 WHAT MOTIVATES YOU?

A. The fear my mom might yell at me. (Alicia, South Africa)

B. Knowing that one day I will grow up to become a woman of substance and valued by my community. (Niyoosha, Pakistan)

C. Deadlines. (Sophie, France)

Your Answer

Friend or Family Answer

82 HOW DO YOU MOTIVATE YOURSELF TO DO SOMETHING YOU NEED TO DO, BUT DON'T WANT TO DO?

A. Counting to seven and then just doing it. (Javier, Mexico)

B. I repeat the consequences of not doing something so that I eventually do it. (Dana, Canada).

C. I try to understand why I should do something. (Pavan, India)

Your Answer

Friend or Family Answer

'DO YOU CONSIDER YOURSELF A PASSIVE, ASSERTIVE, OR AGGRESSIVE PERSON AND WHY?'

83

DO YOU CONSIDER YOURSELF A PASSIVE, ASSERTIVE, OR AGGRESSIVE PERSON AND WHY?

A. Assertive; I tell people what I need. (Eduardo, Peru)

B. I can be assertive at times, but I am mostly passive. (Miu, Japan)

C. I am aggressive. (Brandon, U.S.A.)

Your Answer

Friend or Family Answer

84

WHEN IS IT APPROPRIATE TO BE PASSIVE, ASSERTIVE, OR AGGRESSIVE?

A. I am passive when trouble happens at my school, I don't get involved because then I get in trouble too. (Lilliana, U.S.A.)

B. I am assertive during serious situations. (Dana, Canada).

C. I am aggressive when someone wants me to do something I don't want to do. (Nzemeke, Kenya)

Your Answer

Friend or Family Answer

'IF A MOMENT WENT VIRAL IN YOUR LIFE,
WHAT WOULD IT BE?'

85 IF A MOMENT WENT VIRAL IN YOUR LIFE, WHAT WOULD IT BE?

A. Scoring a winning goal for my team in overtime. (Kyla, U.S.A)

B. When I'm giving an awesome speech at school. (Alicia, South Africa)

C. A surprise party for my dad. (Jaime, Australia)

Your Answer

Friend or Family Answer

86 WHAT IS YOUR FAVORITE TYPE OF VIRAL VIDEOS?

A. Pets doing crazy things. (Rocky, U.S.A.)

B. Pranks. (Niko, Netherlands)

C. Dance moves. (Nusrat, Bangladesh)

Your Answer

Friend or Family Answer

'WHAT IS A SIMPLE PLEASURE?'

87 WHAT IS A SIMPLE PLEASURE?

A. Brushing my teeth. (Kyla, U.S.A)

B. Hanging out with my best friend. (Heitor, Brazil)

C. Eating my favorite food. (Kim, South Korea)

Your Answer

Friend or Family Answer

88 WHAT'S THE BEST WAY TO APPRECIATE SMALL THINGS IN LIFE?

A. By being grateful for all our blessings. (Angel, U.S.A.)

B. By slowing down and noticing what we have already. (Sophie, France)

C. Be present and notice beauty. (Niyoosha, Pakistan)

Your Answer

Friend or Family Answer

'IF ALIENS LANDED, WHAT WOULD YOU ASK THEM?'

89 IF ALIENS LANDED, WHAT WOULD YOU ASK THEM?

A. What took you so long? (Etienne, France)

B. How is your world different from ours? (Javier, Mexico)

C. Can I ride on top? (Kiera, U.S.A.)

Your Answer

Friend or Family Answer

90 DO YOU THINK THEY WOULD BE FRIENDLY? WHY OR WHY NOT?

A. They will probably express dominance and claim our planet as their own. (Pavan, India)

B. They will be nice unless we attack them.
(Yennifer, Dominican Republic)

C. They would probably be grumpy since they traveled from so far away. So, not friendly. (Lisa, U.S.A.)

Your Answer

Friend or Family Answer

'IF YOU COULD BE TRANSPORTED INSIDE A BOOK,
WHICH BOOK WOULD YOU CHOOSE?'

91 IF YOU COULD BE TRANSPORTED INSIDE A BOOK, WHICH BOOK WOULD YOU CHOOSE?

A. Diary of A Wimpy Kid. (George, U.S.A)

B. Alice in Wonderland. (Sophie, France)

C. Harry Potter. (Heitor, Mexico)

Your Answer

Friend or Family Answer

92 IF YOU COULD BE TRANSPORTED INTO A TELEVISION SHOW OR MOVIE, WHICH WOULD YOU CHOOSE?

A. Stranger Things. (Dana, Canada)

B. Sponge Bob Square Pants. (Lisa, U.S.A)

C. Avengers. (Niko, Netherlands)

Your Answer

Friend or Family Answer

'WHAT'S THE LAST TIME YOU ACTED IRRATIONALLY?'

93 WHAT'S THE LAST TIME YOU ACTED IRRATIONALLY?

A. I pushed my sister for no reason. (Kyra, U.S.A.)

B. Once, I just decided to put random answers on my math test. (Eduardo, Peru)

C. The last time I acted irrationally was not talking to a friend because I thought she had been ignoring me. (Niyoosha, Pakistan)

Your Answer

Friend or Family Answer

94 WHEN HAS YOUR HEART TOLD YOU ONE THING AND YOUR MIND TOLD YOU SOMETHING ELSE?

A. Right now, my heart feels I'm in love, but my mind thinks I need to focus on my studies. (Zaidh, Nigeria)

B. My heart wants to skateboard, but my mind wants me to do my homework. (Jaime, Australia)

C. I played in the rain, even though my mind told me that I might get sick. (Sophie, France)

Your Answer

Friend or Family Answer

'WHAT'S THE WORST EXCUSE YOU'VE EVER HEARD
OR GIVEN?'

95 WHAT'S THE WORST EXCUSE YOU'VE EVER HEARD OR GIVEN?

A. One kid said he was late because he got lost on the way to school. (Dana, Canada)

B. My friend said he bumped his head and got amnesia. (Brandon, U.S.A.)

C. I said I hurt my hand and couldn't write. (Etienne, France)

Your Answer

Friend or Family Answer

96 WHEN DO EXCUSES INTERFERE WITH FINDING SOLUTIONS?

A. Excuses birth procrastination and failure. (Zaidh, Nigeria)

B. When the excuse is not true. (Niko, Netherlands)

C. When we give up trying. (Niyoosha, Pakistan)

Your Answer

Friend or Family Answer

'DO YOU THINK THERE WILL BE A TIME IN WHICH
TECHNOLOGY HAS GONE TOO FAR?'

97 DO YOU THINK THERE WILL BE A TIME IN WHICH TECHNOLOGY HAS GONE TOO FAR?

A. If we are 99% robot, yes. (Eduardo, Peru)

B. We have already gone too far. We are destroying the Earth. (Nzemeke, Kenya)

C. It depends on what technology and what we do with it. (Noah, U.S.A.)

Your Answer

Friend or Family Answer

98 WHAT EFFECT WILL TECHNOLOGY HAVE ON THE HUMAN RACE?

A. Robots will take over. (Jaime, Australia)

B. We will live longer, assuming we get enough exercise. (Lisa, U.S.A.)

C. We won't have to leave home. (Javier, U.S.A.)

Your Answer

Friend or Family Answer

'WHAT'S THE CRAZIEST THING YOU HAVE EVER HEARD?'

99 WHAT'S THE CRAZIEST THING YOU HAVE EVER HEARD?

A. My friend told me there is a ghost in his house. (Milka, Montenegro)

B. That the Earth is flat. (Noah, U.S.A.)

C. The Simpsons predicted the future. (Javier, Mexico)

Your Answer

Friend or Family Answer

100 HOW DO YOU KNOW WHAT'S TRUE?

A. Go to trusted websites. (Ettienne, France)

B. I ask my parents. (Kiera, U.SA.)

C. I ask my teachers. (Miu, Japan)

Your Answer

Friend or Family Answer

OTHER BOOKS

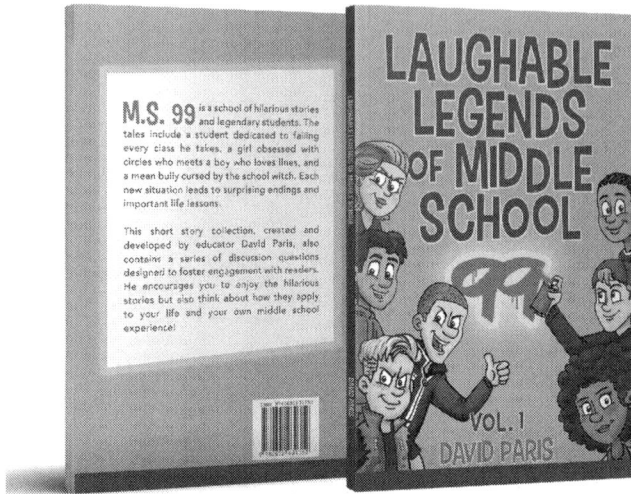

Laughable Legends of Middle School 99

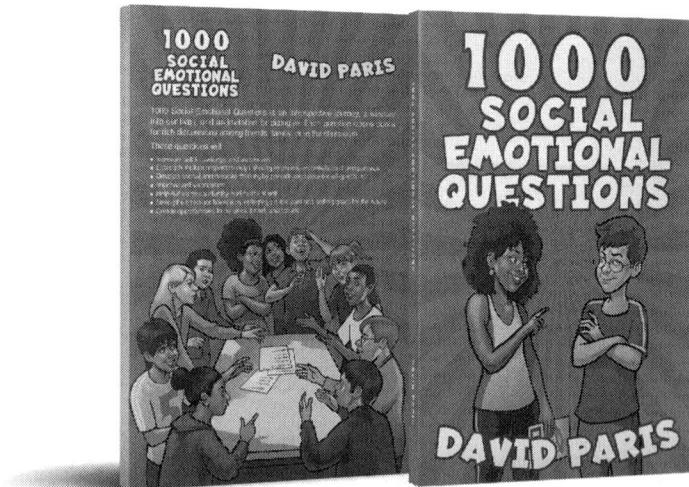

1000 Social Emotional Questions

BY DAVID PARIS

Middle School President

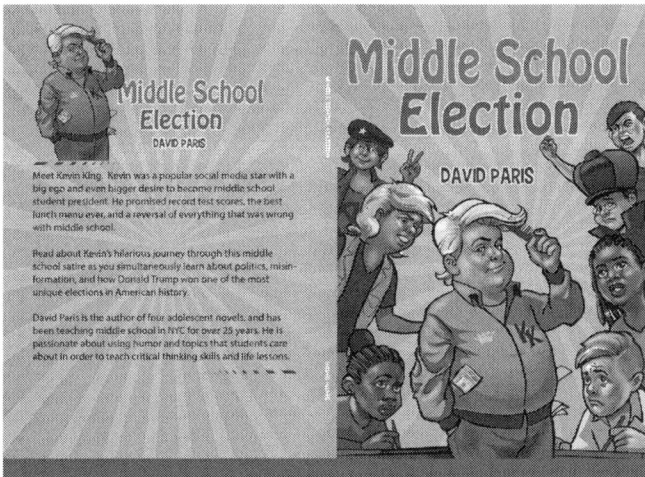

Middle School Election

ABOUT THE AUTHOR

David Paris is an educational consultant and has 30 years of experience teaching in NYC public schools. He is the author of 14 books, he is a group facilitator of Non-Violent Communication (NYCNVC.ORG) and a trainer with Alternative to Violence Program (AVPUSA.Org). David is also a seven-time acrobatic dance champion, co-director of Paradizo Dance, and was a finalist on America's Got Talent.

DavidParisBooks.com

SELLifeSkills.com

ParadizoDance.com

Made in United States
Troutdale, OR
02/10/2025